Harriet Tubman

by Martha E. H. Rustad

Consulting Editor: Gail Saunders-Smith, Ph.D.
Consultant: Evelyn Townsend, President,
Harriet Tubman Organization

Pebble Books

an imprint of Capstone Press
Mankato, Minnesota

Pebble Books are published by Capstone Press
151 Good Counsel Drive, P.O. Box 669, Mankato, Minnesota 56002
http://www.capstone-press.com

1 2 3 4 5 6 07 06 05 04 03 02

Library of Congress Cataloging-in-Publication Data
Rustad, Martha E. H. (Martha Elizabeth Hillman), 1975–
    Harriet Tubman / by Martha E. H. Rustad.
    p. cm.—(First biographies)
    Includes bibliographical references and index.
    ISBN 0-7368-0997-X
    1. Tubman, Harriet, 1820?–1913—Juvenile literature. 2. Slaves—United States—
Biography—Juvenile literature. 3. African American women—Biography—Juvenile
literature. 4. African Americans—Biography—Juvenile literature. 5. Underground
railroad—Juvenile literature. [1. Tubman, Harriet, 1820?–1913. 2. Slaves.
3. Underground railroad. 4. African Americans—Biography. 5. Women—Biography.]
I. Title. II. First biographies (Mankato, Minn.)
E444.T82 R87 2002
305.5′67′092—dc21   2001000264

Summary: Simple text and photographs introduce the life of Harriet Tubman.

Note to Parents and Teachers

The First Biographies series supports national history standards for units on people and culture. This book describes and illustrates the life of Harriet Tubman. The photographs support early readers in understanding the text. This book also introduces early readers to subject-specific vocabulary words, which are defined in the Words to Know section. Early readers may need assistance to read some words and to use the Table of Contents, Words to Know, Read More, Internet Sites, and Index/Word List sections of the book.

Table of Contents

Time Line

early 1820s
born

Harriet Tubman was born in the early 1820s in Maryland. She and her family were slaves. They were not free to choose their jobs or homes.

◀ slaves working in sugarcane field

Time Line

early 1820s
born

late 1820s
begins
working

Slaves had to work hard. Harriet started working when she was about 6 years old. She cleaned the house and worked in the fields.

slaves working in cotton field

Time Line

early 1820s
born

late 1820s
begins
working

Most slaves lived in the southern United States. Slavery was against the law in the northern United States. Some slaves tried to escape to the North.

slaves escaping

Time Line

early 1820s
born

10

late 1820s
begins
working

1849
escapes to
Philadelphia

Harriet escaped in 1849. She traveled to Philadelphia and became free. But Harriet worried about her family and friends. She wanted to help them escape.

 Harriet

Time Line

early 1820s
born

12

late 1820s
begins
working

1849
escapes to
Philadelphia

Harriet became part of the Underground Railroad. Escaping slaves used this system of safe houses. They secretly traveled from one house to another.

slaves on the Underground Railroad

Time Line

early 1820s born	late 1820s begins working	1849 escapes to Philadelphia	1850s leads people on Underground Railroad

Harriet helped many slaves escape during the 1850s. She led about 300 people along the Underground Railroad. Her work was dangerous.

 Harriet (far left)

Time Line

| early 1820s born | late 1820s begins working | 1849 escapes to Philadelphia | 1850s leads people on Underground Railroad |

The North and the South fought the Civil War from 1861 to 1865. Harriet was a cook, a nurse, and a scout for the North. The North won the war. Slavery became against the law in all states.

1861–1865
the Civil War

Time Line

early 1820s
born

late 1820s
begins
working

1849
escapes to
Philadelphia

1850s
leads people
on Underground
Railroad

Harriet moved to New York. She wanted to help black people who were now free. She welcomed them into her home. She raised money to build schools for black children.

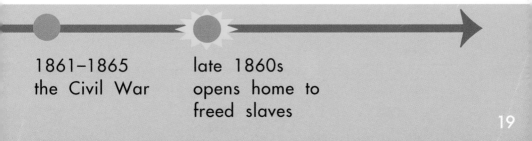

1861–1865
the Civil War

late 1860s
opens home to
freed slaves

early 1820s	late 1820s	1849	1850s
born	begins working	escapes to Philadelphia	leads people on Underground Railroad

Harriet Tubman died in 1913. People remember her for helping many slaves escape to freedom. They also remember her for helping freed slaves live better lives.

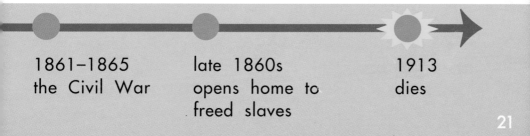

1861–1865
the Civil War

late 1860s
opens home to
freed slaves

1913
dies

Words to Know

Civil War—the U.S. war from 1861 to 1865 between the North and the South; the two sides fought over states' rights.

dangerous—not safe

escape—to break free from a place

freedom—the right to live the way you want

law—a rule made by the government that must be obeyed

safe house—a place where escaping slaves could hide; people who lived in the houses believed slavery was wrong.

scout—someone sent to find and bring back information; some scouts spy on enemies.

slave—a person owned by another person; slaves were not not free to choose their homes or jobs.

Underground Railroad—a series of safe houses and secret routes; many slaves escaped by traveling to the North from one house to another.

Read More

Kulling, Monica. *Escape North!: The Story of Harriet Tubman.* Step into Reading. New York: Random House, 1999.

Lutz, Norma Jean. *Harriet Tubman.* Famous Figures of the Civil War Era. Philadelphia: Chelsea House, 2000.

Sullivan, George. *Harriet Tubman.* In Their Own Words. New York: Scholastic, 2001.

Internet Sites

Aboard the Underground Railroad
http://www.cr.nps.gov/NR/travel/underground/ugrrhome.htm

Harriet Tubman
http://www.incwell.com/Biographies/Tubman.html

Harriet Tubman and the Underground Railroad
http://www2.lhric.org/pocantico/tubman/tubman.html

Index/Word List

Word Count: 239
Early-Intervention Level: 24

Credits
Heather Kindseth, cover designer and illustrator; Linda Clavel, illustrator;
  Kimberly Danger, photo researcher

Archive Photos, 10
CORBIS, 12
Hulton Getty/Archive Photos, 1, 14, 20
North Wind Picture Archives, 4, 8, 16, 18
Photri-Microstock, cover
Stock Montage, 6